Festivals *of the* *World*

RUSSIA

Gareth Stevens Publishing
MILWAUKEE

Written by
HARLINAH WHYTE

Designed by
LOO CHUAN MING

Picture research by
SUSAN JANE MANUEL

First published in North America in 1997 by
Gareth Stevens Publishing
1555 North RiverCenter Drive, Suite 201
Milwaukee, Wisconsin 53212 USA

For a free color catalog describing Gareth
Stevens' list of high-quality books and multimedia
programs, call
1-800-542-2595 (USA)
or 1-800-461-9120 (Canada).
Gareth Stevens Publishing's Fax: (414) 225-0377.
See our catalog, too, on the World Wide Web:
http://gsinc.com

© TIMES EDITIONS PTE LTD 1997
Originated and designed by
Times Books International
an imprint of Times Editions Pte Ltd
Times Centre, 1 New Industrial Road
Singapore 536196
Printed in Singapore

Library of Congress Cataloging-in-Publication Data:
Whyte, Harlinah.
Russia / by Harlinah Whyte.
p. cm. — (Festivals of the world)
Includes bibliographical references and index.
Summary: Describes how the culture of Russia is
reflected in its many festivals, including
International Women's Day, Reindeer Breeders'
Day, and the Russian Winter Arts Festival.
ISBN 0-8368-1936-5 (lib. bdg.)
1. Festivals—Russia (Federation)—Juvenile
literature. 2 Russia (Federation)—Social life and
customs—Juvenile literature. [1. Festivals—Russia
(Federation). 2. Russia (Federation)—Social life
and customs.] I. Title. II. Series.
GT4856.2.A2W48 1997
394.26947—dc21   97-7879

1 2 3 4 5 6 7 8 9 01 00 99 98 97

CONTENTS

4 **Where's Russia?**

6 **When's the Celebration?**

8 **New Year and Christmas**

12 **Patriotic Holidays**

16 **Easter**

20 **Seasonal Festivals**

24 **Sabantui**

26 **Things For You To Do**
★ **Make Babushka dolls**
★ **Make Russian Sweet Treats**

32 **Glossary and Index**

It's Festival Time . . .

Russia is the biggest country in the world. In such a huge country, there's plenty of space for all types of festivals! Russia has a long history and a rich and exciting culture. Right across the country, you can see lively dancing, gorgeous costumes, patriotic singing, painted eggs, reindeer races, and fairy tale characters that come to life. Come and find out! It's festival time in Russia . . .

WHERE'S RUSSIA?

Russia is the biggest country in the world. It stretches right across eastern Europe and northern Asia. Russia has many different landscapes—icy deserts, swamps, mountains, plains, and pine forests. Most Russians live in western Russia. The capital, Moscow, is in this region. The east and north have fewer people.

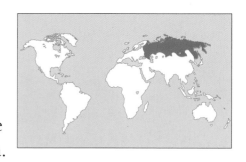

Who are the Russians?

There are many groups of people living within Russia. Most people are Russians, but there are also more than 70 **minority groups**. Each minority group has its own language and customs.

From 1917 to 1991, Russia was part of a huge country called the Soviet Union. The government of the Soviet Union banned many traditions and tried to change the way people lived. After many years of struggle, the Soviet Union broke up in 1991. Russians can once again practice their old customs and traditions.

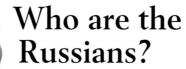

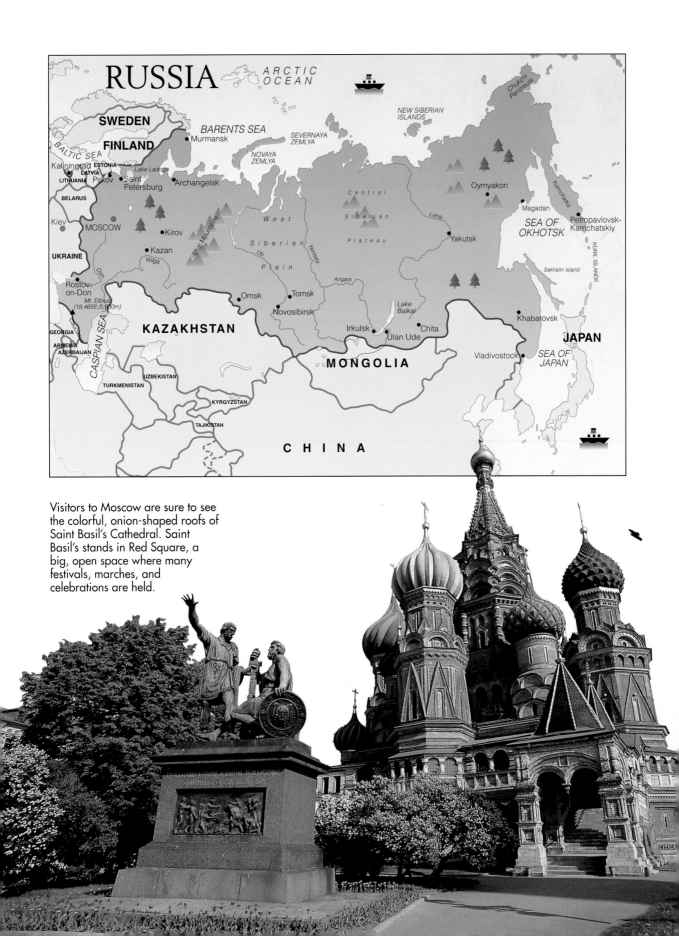

RUSSIA

ARCTIC OCEAN

SWEDEN

FINLAND

BARENTS SEA

Murmansk

SEVERNAYA ZEMLYA

NOVAYA ZEMLYA

NEW SIBERIAN ISLANDS

Chukchi Peninsula

BALTIC SEA

Kaliningrad

ESTONIA

LATVIA

LITHUANIA

Pskov

BELARUS

Lake Ladoga

Saint Petersburg

Archangelsk

Central

Siberian

Plateau

Oymyakon

Magadan

Kamchatka

SEA OF OKHOTSK

Petropavlovsk-Kamchatskiy

Kiev

MOSCOW

Kirov

Ural Mountains

West

Siberian

Plain

Ob

Yenisey

Lena

Yakutsk

KURIL ISLANDS

UKRAINE

Kazan

Volga

Sakhalin Island

Rostov-on-Don

Don

Mt. Elbrus (18,465ft./5,650m)

Omsk

Tomsk

Angara

Lake Baikal

Novosibirsk

Irkutsk

Chita

Khabarovsk

GEORGIA

ARMENIA

AZERBAIJAN

CASPIAN SEA

KAZAKHSTAN

Ulan Ude

Vladivostock

JAPAN

SEA OF JAPAN

UZBEKISTAN

MONGOLIA

TURKMENISTAN

KYRGYZSTAN

TAJIKISTAN

CHINA

Visitors to Moscow are sure to see the colorful, onion-shaped roofs of Saint Basil's Cathedral. Saint Basil's stands in Red Square, a big, open space where many festivals, marches, and celebrations are held.

WHEN'S THE CELEBRATION?

SPRING

- ✪ **INTERNATIONAL WOMEN'S DAY**—Women's work is honored. Men give women flowers, pay them compliments, and perhaps do the housework for a day.
- ✪ **REINDEER BREEDERS' DAY**—Minority groups in the north, including the Yakuts and Nenets, celebrate their culture with reindeer races, herding competitions, singing, and dancing.
- ✪ **SHROVETIDE**—People celebrate the end of winter and prepare for Easter. They eat pancakes and take part in games.
- ✪ **EASTER** ✪ **MAY DAY (SPRING DAY)**
- ✪ **VICTORY DAY** ✪ **SABANTUI**
- ✪ **MAISKIYE ZVEZDY**—An arts festival held in Moscow. This festival's name means "May Stars."

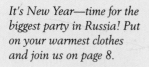

It's New Year—time for the biggest party in Russia! Put on your warmest clothes and join us on page 8.

SUMMER

- ✪ **NATIONAL DAY (INDEPENDENCE DAY)**
- ✪ **YSYAKH**—Festival of the Yakut people that celebrates the driving of their horses to summer pastures.
- ✪ **WHITE NIGHTS FESTIVAL**—Residents of Saint Petersburg enjoy the midnight sun with a festival of music and theater.

Light an Easter candle with me on page 16.

AUTUMN

- ✪ **DAY OF THE CITY**—People in Moscow celebrate their city with games, children's shows, folk parades, and concerts.
- ✪ **OCTOBER REVOLUTION DAY**
- ✪ **HARVEST FESTIVALS**

Toot toot! Come and help us celebrate our national holidays on page 12.

WINTER

- ✪ **NEW YEAR** ✪ **CHRISTMAS**
- ✪ **RUSSIAN WINTER ARTS FESTIVAL**—Russian culture is celebrated with plays, ballets, and musical concerts in Moscow.
- ✪ **WINTER FESTIVALS**

NEW YEAR AND CHRISTMAS

The merriest festival in Russia is the New Year celebration. New Year is followed by Christmas, which is celebrated in Russia on January 7th. From late December until mid-January, Russians enjoy parties, winter sports, and Christmas traditions. Russian children love this time of year— read on and you'll find out why!

Wearing fancy dress at a New Year's party.

Grandfather Frost is a jolly old fellow who looks much like Santa Claus. At this New Year party, there are two Grandfather Frosts, as well as Snow Maiden in her white dress.

Lots of parties!

New Year is a time for parties, especially for children. The biggest parties are held in the Kremlin, an old, red-walled fortress in Moscow. As many as 50,000 children crowd in for each party.

Lively fancy dress parties are held outdoors. Everyone enjoys ice-skating, dancing, and music. Some people are lucky enough to go for a ride on a *troika* [TROY-ka], a sleigh drawn by three horses. The horses are decorated with ribbons, bells, and flowers.

Fairy tales come to life

New Year's parties are sure to be visited by Grandfather Frost and Snow Maiden. These fairy tale characters bring gifts to the children.

Sometimes, the children will also see Babushka in her brightly colored headscarf. According to an old story, Babushka failed to give food and shelter to the three wise men when they were on their journey to visit the Christ Child. People say Babushka still roams the countryside at Christmastime, searching for the Christ Child.

On New Year's Eve, family members gather to drink champagne and wish each other good luck for the coming year. This family is celebrating New Year in Red Square, along with thousands of other Russians. The party goes on all night.

Think about this

In the days following Christmas, Russians read each other's fortunes for the coming year. One way they do this is by dripping candle wax into water and reading the future in the shapes of the thickening wax.

Opposite: These children are enjoying a New Year's party in the park. They have made a puppet for the party.

Village traditions

At Christmastime, children and young people in Russian villages go from home to home singing hymns and Russian folk songs. They praise some local people, and make fun of people who have been selfish or lazy. While singing the songs, the boys throw grain on the steps of their neighbors' houses to wish them a good harvest in the New Year. These are very old traditions that are still practiced today.

Yolka

At this time of year, *yolka* [YOL-kah] can be seen all over town. Yolka are brightly decorated fir trees. New Year's gifts for children, family, and friends are placed under the yolka.

Dancing around the yolka at a New Year's party.

Christmas

Christmas in Russia is a quiet family holiday. On Christmas Eve, many Christians eat nothing all day. When the first star appears at night, families light candles and lamps and sit down to a festive Christmas supper. The most important Christmas dishes are *kutya* [KOOT-yah] (wheat porridge with honey or sugar), and compote (stewed apples, pears, plums, or other fruit). After the festive supper, children usually visit their godparents. They bring along kutya and pies and receive gifts in return.

PATRIOTIC HOLIDAYS

During the days of the Soviet Union, all religious festivals were banned. Instead, new festivals were created. Many are still celebrated in Russia today. These festivals commemorate important events in Russia's history and honor the lives of ordinary citizens. The biggest and most spectacular festivities are held in Red Square in Moscow. So march down to Red Square and join the celebration!

This little girl in uniform is attending the Victory Day parade in Moscow. People of all ages gather in Red Square to honor those who died in World War II. For the soldiers who survived the war, it is a chance to wear all their medals and talk about old times with their friends.

Victory Day

A young couple performs a Russian dance at the Victory Day festivities.

On May 9th, Victory Day commemorates the end of World War II in Europe in 1945. This is Russia's most popular patriotic holiday, but as one poet said, it is "a feast with tears in your eyes." At official celebrations or family gatherings, people observe a minute's silence to honor the 27 million Russians who died in the war.

The holiday brings back sad memories of war, but it is also a day for celebrating Russia's survival. Dancers, singers, and musicians in traditional dress show their pride in their country. In the evening, gun salutes are fired in honor of the fallen soldiers. Television channels show films about the war so that Russians will remember the courage of the soldiers and the suffering of ordinary people.

Soldiers place flowers on a memorial to those who died in the war.

May Day

May 1st is May Day. For hundreds of years, people in Europe have celebrated spring on May 1st. But in some countries, including Russia, May Day is also a day to honor workers.

During the Soviet era, the May Day parade was meant to demonstrate the Soviet Union's military strength. Red Square was filled with soldiers, tanks, and people waving flags.

Today, the marches are less political. Many people now call this holiday Spring Day. Families enjoy the chance to get together and celebrate spring after the long, cold winter.

This picture shows how patriotic holidays were celebrated in the Soviet Union. Thousands of people are marching in Red Square. They are carrying pictures of political leaders.

Today, people show their patriotism by dressing up in national costumes and performing traditional songs and dances.

National Days

November 7th is the anniversary of the October Revolution. The October Revolution in 1917 led to the formation of the Soviet Union. This holiday used to be called National Day.

June 12th is the new National Day. It is also called Independence Day. The new holiday celebrates Russia's independence in 1991.

Both holidays are marked with parades and official meetings and dinners.

Think about this

Victory Day, October Revolution Day, and Independence Day remind people of important events in Russian history. Do you know of any other holidays based on historical events? Why are those events important?

Big papier-mâché puppets roam the streets on May Day, Victory Day, and other holidays.

Celebrating Russian culture

Russians are very proud of their rich culture. Russian composers, artists, and writers have produced some of the world's great masterpieces.

On national holidays, there are many performances of Russian ballet, music, and theater. Sometimes the performances are free. This gives everybody, rich and poor, a chance to enjoy the best of Russian culture.

People from minority groups also celebrate their culture on national holidays. Singers, dancers, and musicians come from all over Russia to perform in Moscow. By sharing their songs and dances with people in the capital, they proclaim their pride in their culture.

15

Beautiful Easter eggs

Russian Easter eggs are famous throughout the world. Decorated eggs are called *pysanky* [pi-SAHN-kee]. They are given as gifts and displayed through the year. Some pysanky are painted. Others are made by dripping melted wax onto an egg and drawing or carving symbols into the wax. Common symbols are ribbons, fishes, crosses, triangles, and stars. When the egg is dipped in dye, the part of the shell covered by wax is not affected by the dye. More drawing or carving is done on the wax, and the egg is again dipped in dye, but this time using another color. Decorating eggs is an art that requires much practice and patience.

The pysanky on the left and in the center have been painted. The two on the right have been decorated with wax and then dipped in dye. Can you tell the difference? On page 26 you can read about the most valuable Easter eggs in the world.

These people have brought their kulich to the church to be blessed by the priest. The kulich are decorated with candles, flowers, and painted eggs.

Try some kulich!

Russian women bake a delicious cake called *kulich* [KOO-lich] for the Easter celebration. Friends and relatives exchange the big, round cakes, which are packed with raisins, nuts, and candied fruit. Sometimes this turns into a friendly competition to see who can make the most delicious kulich. Before the festive meal on Easter Sunday, the kulich is taken to the church to be blessed.

The festive meal

After the midnight church service and procession, the family goes home to enjoy an Easter feast. Many Russian Christians **fast** for 40 days before Easter, so the Easter feast is a very special celebration. The table is set with kulich, decorated eggs, and lots of delicious food.

During the meal, children and grown-ups play a game with painted hard-boiled eggs. They each take an egg and knock them together. The person whose egg doesn't crack is the winner!

Remembering the dead

On Easter Sunday, many Russians visit the graves of friends and relatives who have died. They put a painted egg and a slice of kulich on the grave. Some people even drink a glass of **vodka** to honor the dead.

Visiting graves on Easter Sunday is not really a Christian tradition. The Russian Orthodox Church says that Easter should be a day of rejoicing at Jesus Christ's resurrection, not a time to remember the dead. But many Russians still like to honor the dead at Easter time.

Outside the church on Easter Day, the priest uses a brush to sprinkle holy water on the crowd of worshipers.

19

SEASONAL FESTIVALS

Throughout the year, Russians celebrate many festivals to mark the changing seasons. In spring, people celebrate the return of sunshine and warm weather. Summer and autumn are the time for harvest festivals. The winters are long and cold—perfect for snow festivals! Russians have found ways to enjoy every season of the year. There's never a bad time for a festival in Russia!

Opposite: A cheerful straw figure representing the spirit of winter is burned to welcome the spring.

Below: Three **Chukchi** girls and their Russian friends are dressed up for the Chukchi spring festival. The Chukchi live in northeastern Russia. The tip of the Chukchi Peninsula is only a few miles from Alaska. In this freezing region, the end of winter is a time for them to celebrate!

Spring—at last!

After a long winter, Russians look forward to the warm days ahead. There are spring festivals all over the country. In some places, people build a straw figure representing the spirit of winter. They burn the figure to chase away winter and welcome the spring. Spring and summer are important seasons for farmers, so there are lots of country festivals that celebrate the sowing of crops and the moving of animals to summer pastures.

On the Kamchatka Peninsula in far eastern Russia, it's still cold at the beginning of spring. Wrapped in thick fur jackets, these children are enjoying the spring festival with their puppet friends.

Time for the harvest

In summer and autumn, harvest festivals are held in towns and villages. Houses are decorated with flower wreaths and sheaves of corn and wheat. Baskets filled with grain, vegetables, and fruit are put up in the main street or village square. Sometimes people dress up as folk characters representing the spirit of the local crops, such as "Wheat" or "Corn." Singers wear traditional dress and sing praise to the harvest. There is music and dancing until late in the evening.

When the first wheat has been harvested, Russian villagers grind it into flour and use it to bake bread. The huge loaves are brought to the harvest parade, along with baskets of fruit and seeds for the next planting.

Festivals of snow and ice

Despite the icy weather and the short days, Russians love winter. All that snow and ice is perfect for skiing, reindeer racing, and . . . swimming? In northwestern Russia, people cut holes in the ice and take a dip in the freezing cold water beneath. Others carve ice sculptures, go ice-skating, and enjoy sleigh rides. Whole towns and fortresses are built of snow. Teams fight mock battles, defending their snow forts from fierce snowball attacks.

Think about this
Many seasonal festivals honor the crops and animals that people depend on for survival. There are festivals that honor horses, reindeer, potatoes, apples, tomatoes, and corn.

In this exciting race, a man wearing skis is being pulled along by reindeer.

Swimming is no joke when it's this cold! The swimmers are wearing shoes and boots so their feet don't freeze while they are waiting to jump in.

SABANTUI

The **Tatars** live in southwestern Russia, around the city of Kazan. Each spring they celebrate an agricultural festival called Sabantui, which means "Feast of the Plow." This celebration of Tatar culture is a chance for people to show off their skills at traditional sports, singing, dancing, and cooking.

The aim of this contest is to knock the other person off the log!

Horse races and wrestling

The Tatars were originally **nomads**. Horses were essential for moving people and their belongings from place to place. Horse races are still one of the highlights of Sabantui.

The Tatars are also great wrestlers. The bouts at Sabantui are fiercely contested. The wrestlers grab each other by the belt and try to throw each other to the ground. Young girls present the strongest and most skillful winners with gifts—usually traditional embroidered towels.

There are also lots of light-hearted contests, from running races to egg-and-spoon races.

24

Fun for everyone!

When people are tired from all the racing and wrestling, there are plenty of other festivities to enjoy. Cooks compete to produce the best national dishes. Musicians surround the cooks and play folk songs to keep everyone entertained. In the evening, the young people stage open-air shows. Anyone can take part in the song and dance competitions, and no one goes home without a prize or gift.

A man proves his strength by carrying a sheep on his shoulders.

Children don't miss out on the spring games. These boys are competing in a tug of war contest.

THINGS FOR YOU TO DO

Russians have produced some of the world's greatest works of art, ballet, music, and literature. This cultural wealth is celebrated on national holidays and at arts festivals, such as the Russian Winter Arts Festival in Moscow and the White Nights Festival in Saint Petersburg. Come and learn about some of the masterpieces of Russian culture.

Fabergé eggs

Russians love to give and receive Easter eggs. The most famous and valuable Easter eggs in the world were made by Peter Carl Fabergé [FAB-er-zhay]. Fabergé was a jeweler from Saint Petersburg. In 1884, the **tsar** [zar] of Russia, Alexander III, asked Fabergé to make a special Easter egg for his wife. For the next 23 years, Fabergé made Easter eggs for the royal family. The eggs were made with gold and precious jewels. Many of them opened up to reveal a surprise—a tiny basket of flowers, a little statue, or a series of portraits of the tsar's family.

This golden Fabergé egg is a clock. The white band moves around the egg so the arrow points at the time.

Learn about ballet

Russian ballet is considered the best in the world. Russian dancers are known for their discipline, grace, and dramatic performance style. Some of the greatest ballet dancers in history came from Russia. The most famous are Vaslav Nijinsky, Anna Pavlova, and Rudolf Nureyev.

There are two main ballet companies in Russia—the Bolshoi Ballet in Moscow and the Maryinsky (or Kirov) Ballet in Saint Petersburg. These companies have toured abroad and performed to audiences all over the world. If you're lucky, you may be able to see them perform. Otherwise, you can watch their performances on video and read about them in books. Perhaps you might even like to learn ballet yourself!

They make it look easy, but these Russian dancers have practiced hard to develop strength and balance.

Things to look for in your library

Christmas in Russia. (Passport Books, 1993).

The Empire of the Czars. Esther Carrion (Children's Press, 1996).

Imperial Surprises: A Pop-up Book of Fabergé Masterpieces. Margaret Kelly (Harry N. Abrams, 1994).

The People of Russia and their Food. Ann L. Burckhardt (Capstone Press, 1996).

Postcards from Russia. Helen Arnold (Raintree/Steck-Vaughn, 1995).

Russia Today: Its Land and People. (United Learning video).

Russian Girl: Life in an Old Russian Town. Russ Kendall (Scholastic Trade, 1994).

Teach Me Russian (book and tape of songs in Russian). Judy Mahoney (Teach Me Tapes, 1991).

MAKE BABUSHKA DOLLS

Christmas is the perfect time for Russian children to play with Babushka dolls. Each Babushka doll fits inside the next. They are usually made from wood, but here's an easy way to make your own.

You will need:
1. 1 large can
2. 1 medium can
3. 1 small can
4. A can opener
5. 3–4 tablespoons flour
6. A bowl
7. Newspaper
8. Scissors
9. A pencil
10. Paints
11. A paint tray
12. Paintbrushes

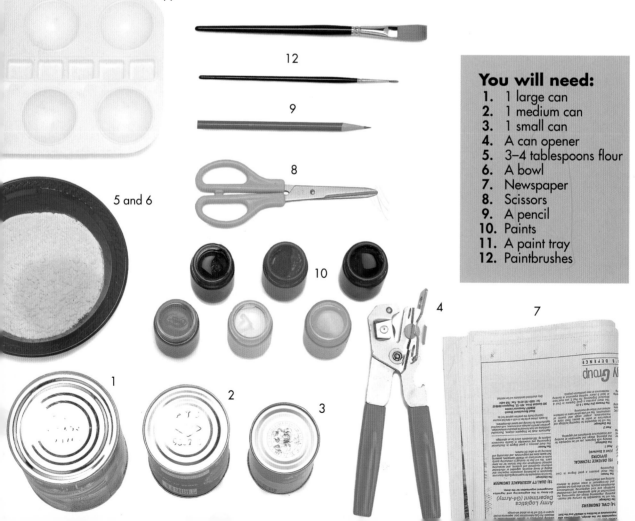

1 Use the can opener to remove one lid from each can. The edges are sharp, so have an adult help you. The cans should be empty and clean.

3 Dip a newspaper strip into the paste and stick it onto a can. Continue smoothing on strips until the lid and sides of the can are covered with two or three layers of papier-mâché. When you have covered all three cans, leave them to dry.

4 When the cans are completely dry, draw Babushka's face, scarf, and dress patterns onto the cans. Finish off the decoration with colorful paints.

MAKE RUSSIAN SWEET TREATS

Russians enjoy sweet food at many of their festivals. You can make these sweet treats yourself. When you bite into them, you get a sudden taste of the sugar, walnut, and cinnamon filling. They're delicious!

You will need:

1. ½ cup (80 g) unsalted butter, softened
2. 4 oz. (120 g) cream cheese, softened
3. 1 cup (120 g) flour
4. ⅛ teaspoon salt
5. ½ cup (60 g) chopped walnuts
6. ¼ cup (30 g) sugar
7. 1 teaspoon cinnamon
8. Extra flour
9. A large mixing bowl
10. A small mixing bowl
11. Measuring cups
12. Measuring spoons
13. A wooden spoon
14. A plate
15. Aluminum foil
16. A rolling pin
17. A cutting board
18. A spoon
19. A knife
20. A baking tray
21. Potholders

1 Combine the butter and cream cheese in the large mixing bowl. Stir until completely combined. Add the flour and salt. Mix well.

2 Shape the dough into seven balls. Put them on a dinner plate, cover with aluminum foil, and put into the refrigerator for several hours.

3 Lightly dust your cutting board with some flour. Roll the balls into 6 inch (15 cm) circles. Cut each circle into quarters.

4 In the small mixing bowl, combine the walnuts, sugar, and cinnamon. Drop a rounded teaspoon of this mixture onto each quarter of the dough. To close the cookie, pinch together the edges of the dough to form a triangle. Place the cookies on an ungreased baking tray. Bake at 350°F (180°C) for 15 minutes, or until lightly browned. Makes 28 sweet treats.

GLOSSARY

censer, 17 — A container in which incense is burned.

Chukchi, 20 — A minority group in the far northeast of Russia.

fast, 19 — Eating no food, or only some kinds of food, for a period of time.

icon, 16 — A religious painting of Jesus Christ or a saint.

kulich, 18 — A big Easter cake filled with raisins, nuts, and candied fruit.

kutya, 11 — Sweet porridge eaten at Christmas.

minority group, 4 — A group of people whose religion, customs, or race is different from that of most people in the population.

nomads, 24 — People who move from place to place in a group, searching for pasture or food. They have no permanent home.

pysanky, 18 — Decorated Easter eggs.

Tatars, 24 — A minority group in southwestern Russia.

tsar, 26 — A Russian emperor. The last tsar ruled until 1917.

troika, 9 — A sleigh pulled by a team of three horses.

vodka, 19 — A strong alcoholic drink made from potato, rye, or wheat mash.

yolka, 11 — A decorated fir tree.

INDEX

Babushka, 9, 28
ballet, 15, 27

Christmas, 8, 9, 11

Easter, 16–19, 26

Fabergé eggs, 26

Grandfather Frost, 8, 9

Independence Day (National Day), 15

Kremlin, 9

May Day (Spring Day), 14

minority groups, 4, 15
Moscow, 4, 5, 9, 12, 15, 26, 27

New Year, 8–11

October Revolution Day, 15

Red Square, 5, 9, 12, 14, 17
reindeer races, 23
Russian Orthodox Church, 16, 19
Russian sweet treats, 30–31

Sabantui, 24–25
Saint Basil's Cathedral, 5
seasonal festivals, 20–23
Snow Maiden, 8, 9

Soviet Union, 4, 12, 14, 15

Victory Day, 12, 13, 15

Picture Credits
Axiom: 2, 12, 13 (both), 14 (bottom), 16 (both), 17; Focus Team, Italy: Title page, 3 (right), 4, 5, 22 (bottom); Haga Library, Japan: 8 (both), 10, 11; Hutchison Library: 9, 19, 20, 22 (top), 27; Life File: 3 (bottom), 18 (top), 28; Mikhail Idamkin: 18 (bottom), 21; Novosti: 6, 14 (top), 26; Travel Ink: 3 (top), 15; Trip: 7 (both), 23 (both), 24, 25 (both)